This NuNubian Book belongs to:

....

....

....

....

Dedicated to all our precious divine children

"Africa is our center of gravity, our cultural and spiritual mother and father,
our beating heart,
no matter where we live on the face of this earth."
Honourable Dr John Henrik Clarke

First published 2014 by
NuNubian Books

Printed in USA by createspace

ISBN 978-0-9930534-0-5

www.nunubianbooks.com

Why I love myself?

N. U. Nubian

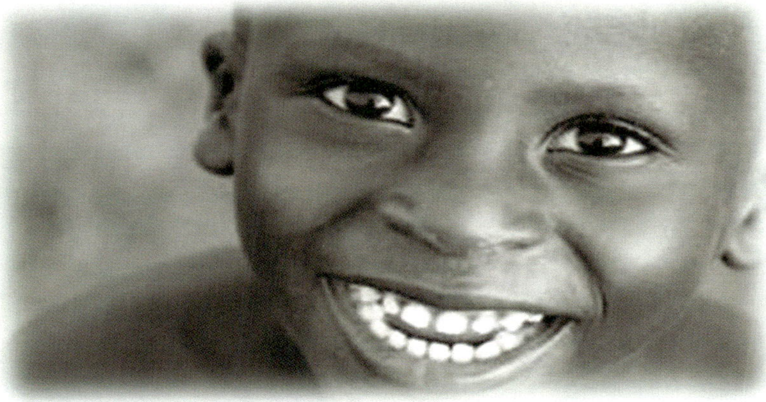

I LOVE my eyes...

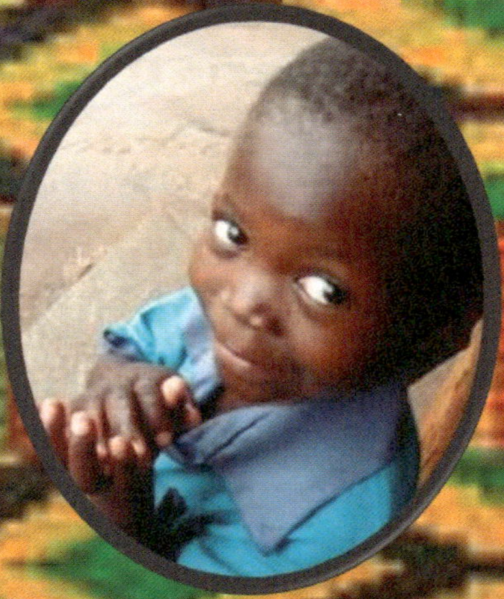

because they are *beautifully brown*

and allow me to *seeeeeeeee*

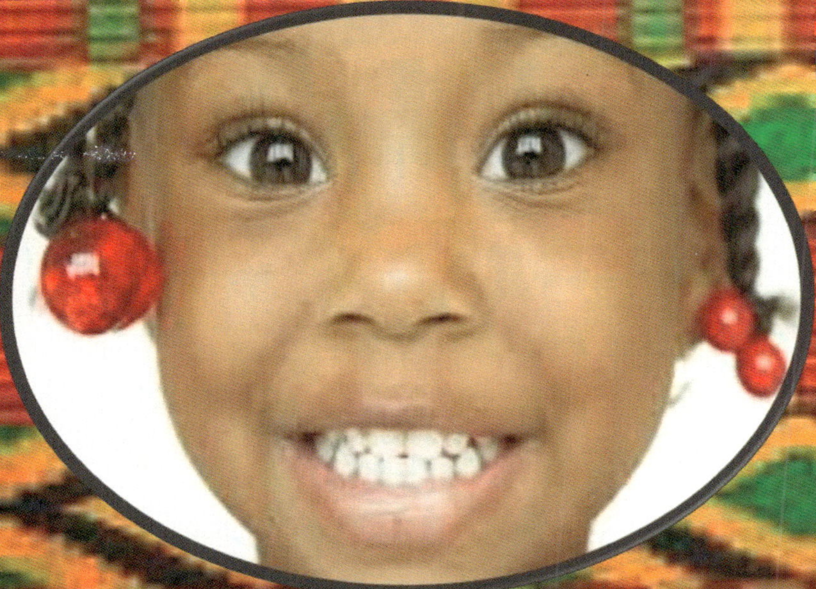

the world around me!

I **LOVE** my ears...

because I can hear Daddy and Mummy
say *wise and wonderful words to me.*

I **LOVE** my

NOSE...

because it allows me to breathe
when it is

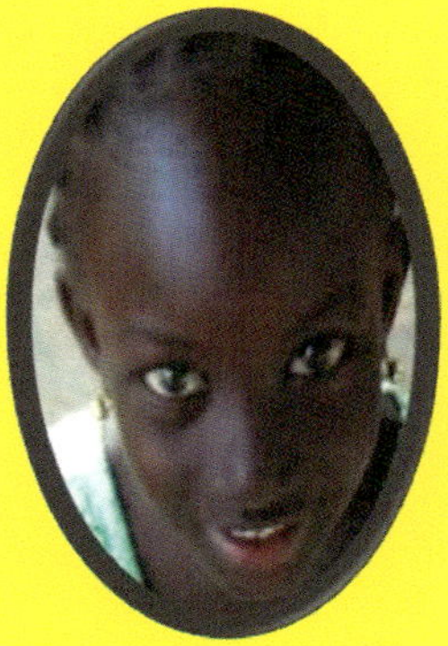

h-h-h-h-hot

and

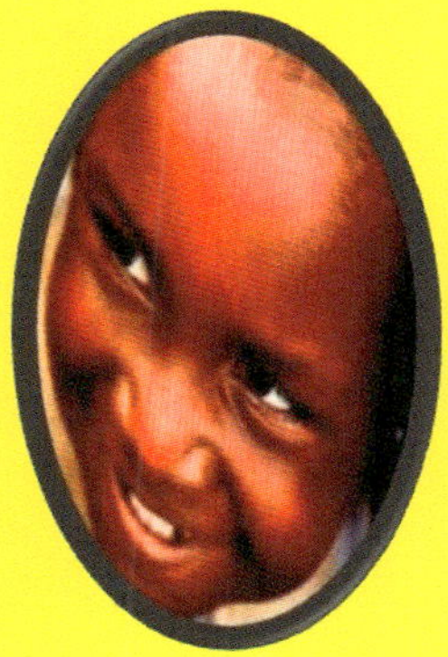
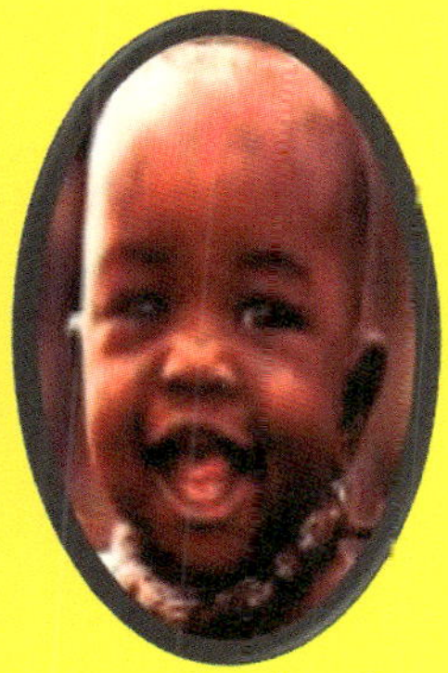

c-c-c-c-cold.

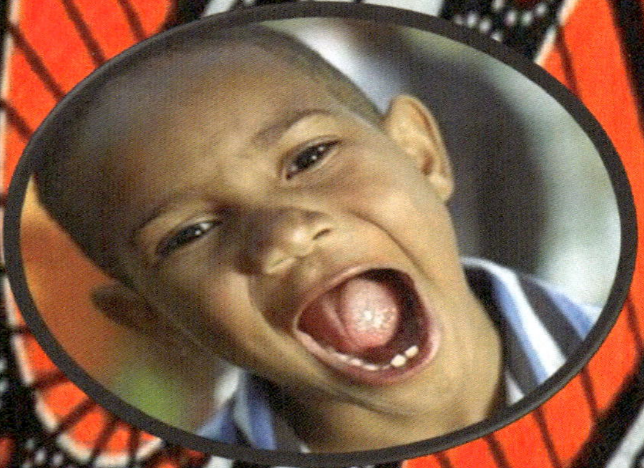

I LOVE my tongue...

because I can taste all my fabulous food and enjoy each *deliciously, delightful bite.*

mm mm MMMMMMMM!!!

I LOVE my lips...

because they are the *best big lips ever*

and

they do

look *gorgeously*

good,

on me.

MWAH!!!

I LOVE my teeth...

they are *super shiny* and
dazzlingly bright,

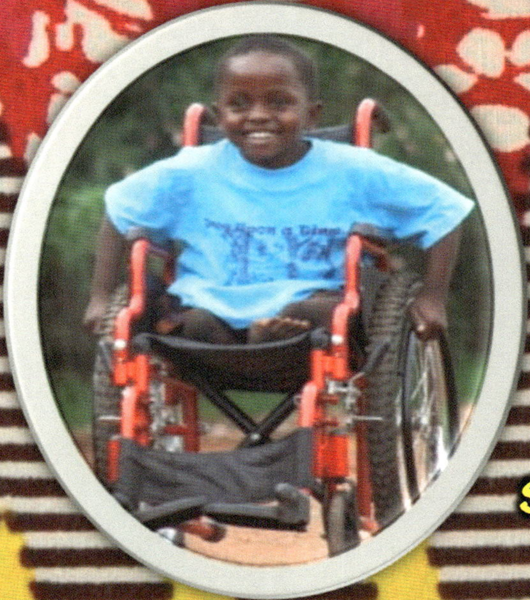

so I can eat with them!

I LOVE my mouth...

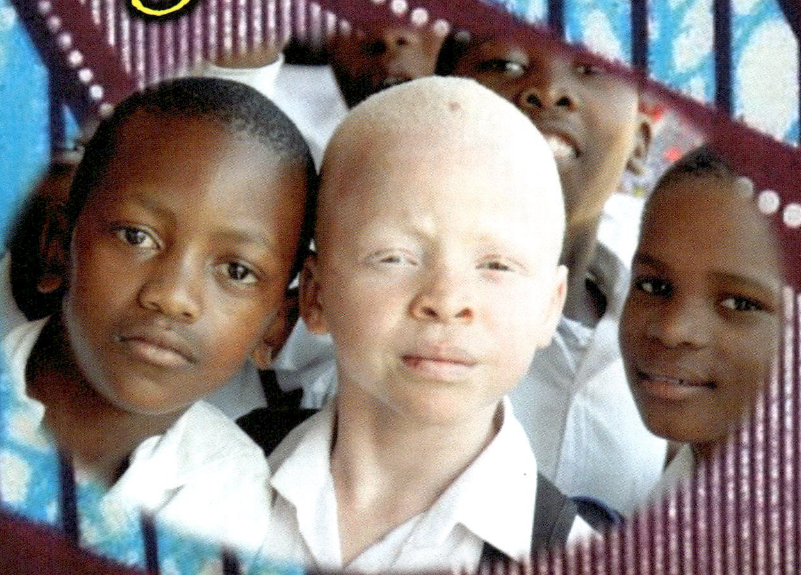

because I can *talk with it*
and laugh with it,
as much as I like.

I LOVE my hands...

because I can *touch gently, really feel*

and clap for myself!
Yeaaaaahhhh!!!

I LOVE my

feet...

because I can walk, run, jump

and

land safely with my knees bent.

Pheww!

I LOVE my

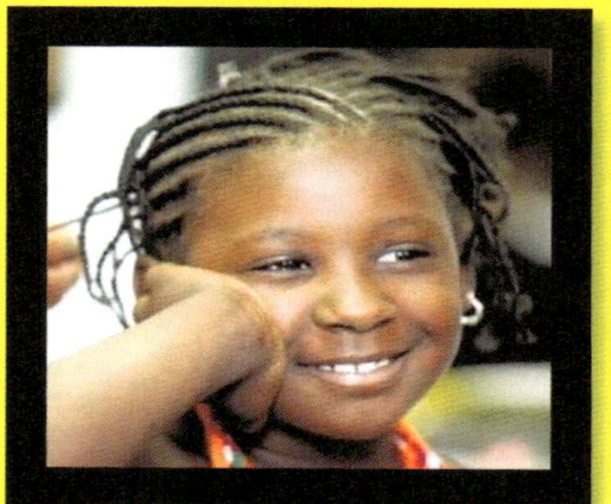

HAIR...

because it is a *regal crown*,

on,

my,

head.

I LOVE my skin...

because it protects me *from*

the rain,

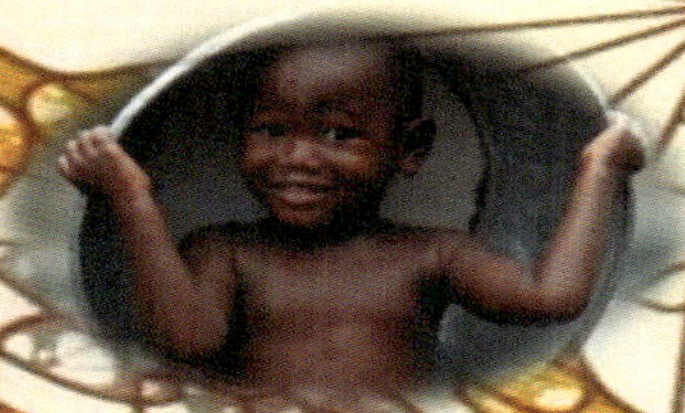

the wind

and the sunshine!!!

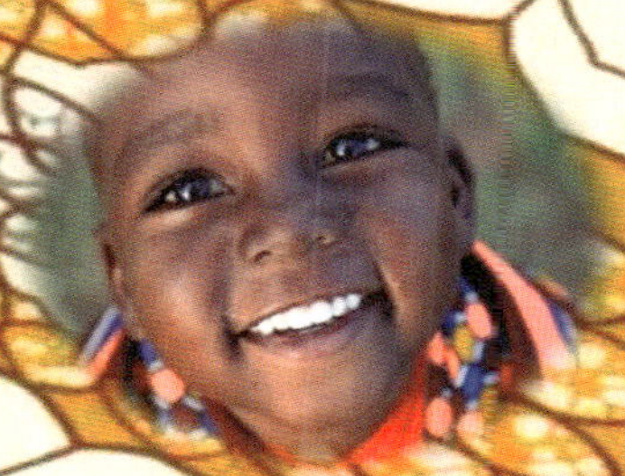

I LOVE my

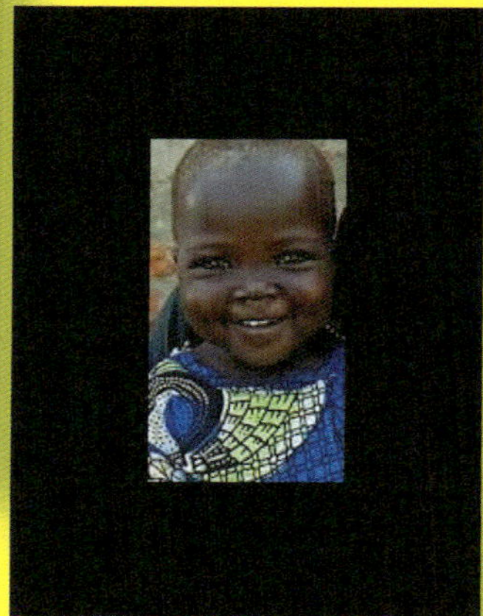

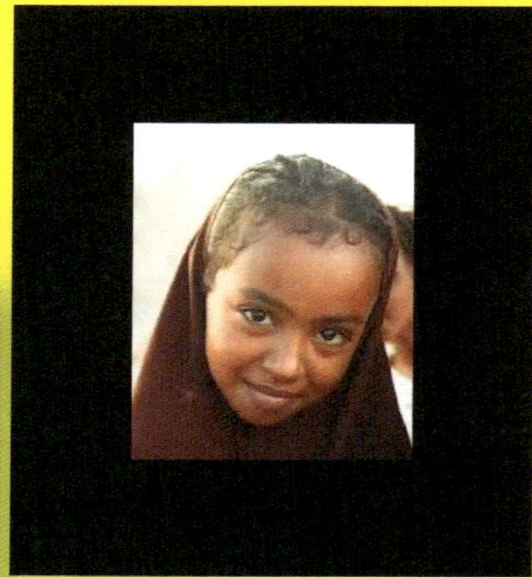

complexion...

because of it's perfect natural colour

and
very
healthy

and
glorious
glow.

I LOVE
my thoughts...

because they are soo
creatively clever
and
I can choose from all the different
feelings, that come from love or fear.

You can choose how to feel, it's all up to you!

I **LOVE** my

inner spirit...

because it is my
real,
energetic
and
powerful self.

I LOVE

myself...

basically because,

I am,

MAJESTIC

ME!!!

STOP!!!

this book is not finished yet...

It is only just beginning?

N. U. Nubian

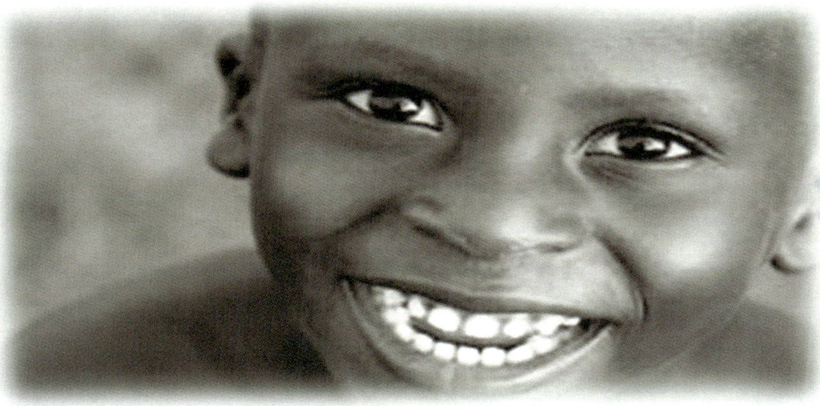

Now *YOU* can create your own

Why I love myself? book

right here...

and here!

NuNubian books are authentically African children's books. Using only the most positive photographs and artwork, to create our own uniquely captivating, meaningful and holistic reading experience. Our books, are to be enjoyed and treasured by al l children, of all ages, from birth to young Kings and Queens. As your child develops and grows, our books will forever be lovingly remembered and revisited, time, after time, after time, again...

WELCOME TO THE NUNUBIAN BOOKS FAMILY